Read for a Better World™

CRANES
A First Look

ZELDA WAGNER

Lerner Publications ◆ Minneapolis

Educator Toolbox

Reading books is a great way for kids to express what they're interested in. Before reading this title, ask the reader these questions:

- What do you think this book is about? Look at the cover for clues.
- What do you already know about cranes?
- What do you want to learn about cranes?

Let's Read Together

Encourage the reader to use the pictures to understand the text.

Point out when the reader successfully sounds out a word.

Praise the reader for recognizing sight words such as *up* and *in*.

TABLE OF CONTENTS

Cranes 4

You Connect! 21
STEM Snapshot 22
Photo Glossary 23
Learn More 23
Index 24

Cranes

Cranes lift things.
They go up high.

Why might cranes lift high?

Workers sit in the cab.

The crane's arm moves.

A hook grabs things. It holds onto them.

The crane picks up a beam. It sets the beam in place.

What do you think cranes help build?

Some trucks have cranes.

Cranes go over bumpy ground.

Why might cranes go over bumpy ground?

Some cranes are tall.

Tall cranes help make buildings. They lift things high.

Cranes lift things with their long arms. They help do tall jobs.

You Connect!

Have you ever seen a crane?

Would you want to drive a crane?

How can you learn more about cranes?

STEM Snapshot

Encourage students to think and ask questions like scientists. Ask the reader:

What is something you learned about cranes?

What is something you noticed about crane parts?

What is something you still want to learn about cranes?

Photo Glossary

Learn More

Alinas, Marv. *Cranes*. Parker, CO: Child's World, 2023.

Pettiford, Rebecca. *Cranes*. Minneapolis: Jump!, 2023.

Wagner, Zelda. *Front-End Loaders: A First Look*. Minneapolis: Lerner Publications, 2025.

Index

arm, 8, 20
cab, 6
hook, 9
lift, 4, 18, 20
tall, 16, 18, 20
truck, 12

Photo Acknowledgments

Image credits: Anton Petrus/Getty Images, p. 5; kali9/Getty Images, p. 6; fermate/Getty Images, p. 7; AerialPerspective Images/Getty Images, p. 8; teptong/Getty Images, p. 9; HHakim/Getty Images, p. 11; Andyqwe/Getty Images, p. 13; Vova Shevchuk/Shutterstock, p. 15; Евгений Харитонов/Getty Images, p. 17; fotog/Getty Images, p. 18; Jordan Lye/Getty Images, p. 19; Twenty47studio/Getty Images, p. 20.
Cover: Cavan Images/Getty Images.

Copyright © 2025 by Lerner Publishing Group, Inc.

All rights reserved. International copyright secured. No part of this book may be reproduced, stored in a retrieval system, or transmitted in any form or by any means—electronic, mechanical, photocopying, recording, or otherwise—without the prior written permission of Lerner Publishing Group, Inc., except for the inclusion of brief quotations in an acknowledged review.

Lerner Publications Company
An imprint of Lerner Publishing Group, Inc.
241 First Avenue North
Minneapolis, MN 55401 USA

For reading levels and more information, look up this title at www.lernerbooks.com.

Main body text set in Mikado Medium.
Typeface provided by Hannes von Doehren.

Library of Congress Cataloging-in-Publication Data

Names: Wagner, Zelda, 2000- author.
Title: Cranes : a first look / Zelda Wagner.
Description: Minneapolis : Lerner Publications, [2025] | Series: Read about construction vehicles | Includes bibliographical references and index. | Audience: Ages 5-8 | Audience: Grades K-1 | Summary: "How do construction workers lift heavy objects? They use a crane! From short homes to tall skyscrapers, readers learn how cranes help with big jobs"— Provided by publisher.
Identifiers: LCCN 2024008847 (print) | LCCN 2024008848 (ebook) | ISBN 9798765647837 (lib. bdg.) | ISBN 9798765662212 (pbk.) | ISBN 9798765657232 (epub)
Subjects: LCSH: Cranes, derricks, etc.—Juvenile literature.
Classification: LCC TJ1363 .W245 2025 (print) | LCC TJ1363 (ebook) | DDC 621.8/73—dc23/eng/20240314

LC record available at https://lccn.loc.gov/2024008847
LC ebook record available at https://lccn.loc.gov/2024008848

Manufactured in the United States of America
1-1010889-53344-5/22/2024